The Circle of Life

by Kristi McGee

Harcourt
SCHOOL PUBLISHERS

W9-BPK-304

Everything goes through a growth process. Puppies, kittens, and human babies grow. They get older. They change along the way. Babies turn into children. Children turn into teenagers. Teenagers turn into adults. These are big changes.

However, these changes aren't as big as the changes in the life of a silkworm. A silkworm changes from a tiny egg to a moth. There are four steps: egg, caterpillar, cocoon, and moth.

STEP 1: Egg

Total Egg Time: 10–14 Days

Think of a chicken egg. The eggshell keeps the chick safe while it grows. When it is ready, the chick breaks out of its shell. The silkworm does the same thing. The silkworm is much smaller than a chick, though. A silkworm's egg is the size of a pinhead! The shell of the egg protects the growing worm.

A silkworm moth lays hundreds of eggs. They are yellow. The eggs rest in cold temperatures. Then the eggs are warmed. Sometimes they get warm as spring comes. If the silkworms are raised by humans, people warm, or incubate, the eggs. Warming makes the eggs change color. They turn blue-gray. Then the eggs start to grow. Two weeks later, tiny silkworms hatch from the eggs.

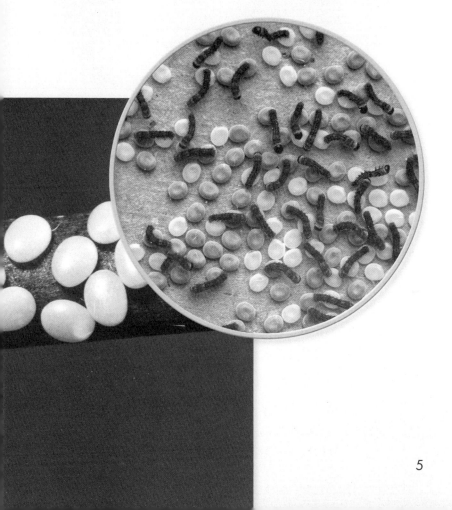

STEP 2: **Caterpillar**

Total Caterpillar Time: 27 Days

   A silkworm is very tiny when it hatches from the egg. It is a caterpillar, or worm. It is only about 1 or 0.04-0.08 inches (1–2 mm) long. That's smaller than a grain of rice.

   In the next twenty-seven days, the caterpillar grows to about 3.15 inches (80 mm). That is eighty times bigger than when it hatched! Imagine if humans grew that much. We would be over 100 feet (30.5 m) tall! That's the size of a ten-story building!

The caterpillar has to eat a lot to grow that much. The only things that the young caterpillars eat are mulberry leaves. The mulberry is a kind of bush or tree. The little caterpillars eat new leaves. The bigger caterpillars eat bigger leaves. If the caterpillars are being raised by people, they are fed special food if mulberry leaves are not available.

The caterpillar changes as it grows. In fact, it sheds its skin four times. This is called molting. Other animals molt, too. Have you ever seen a snakeskin? Snakes lose their skin just like silkworms. Even birds molt. They don't lose skin. They lose feathers. Sometimes the caterpillars eat their own skin.

What does a silkworm caterpillar look like? It is gray in color. Its body is in segments, or parts. The head and first segment of a caterpillar can swell and look bigger. This helps scare off enemies. A full-grown caterpillar looks glossy, or shiny. It is full of silk.

STEP 3: Cocoon

Total Cocoon Time: 14 Days

Building a cocoon is hard work. The cocoon is made out of silk. The silk comes out of the caterpillar near its mouth. First, the caterpillar has to find a good place to build its cocoon. The cocoon will be held in place by silk. The caterpillar attaches the silk to a safe place. Then, the caterpillar starts making its cocoon. Each caterpillar has nearly 15 inches (38.1 cm) of silk inside its body! That's a lot for a 3-inch (7.6 cm) caterpillar.

The caterpillar moves its head back and forth to make the cocoon. The silkworm makes the cocoon in two or three days. Finally, the silkworm is closed inside the waterproof cocoon. Big changes take place inside the cocoon. The caterpillar molts one last time. Its body turns hard and brown. Then it starts changing into a moth.

STEP 4: Moth

Total Moth Time: 5–7 Days

The moth grows inside the cocoon. When the moth is ready to come out, it weakens the cocoon. The moth uses its saliva to do this. The moth comes out ready to lay eggs. Silkworm moths are about 2 inches (5.1 cm) wide. The moths are light tan or gray. They cannot fly or eat. Their mouths aren't totally formed. The moths live for only a few days after laying eggs. Then the moths die. The silkworm's life cycle begins again.

Total Life Cycle of a Silkworm: 62 Days

All About the Silk

People don't make silk material from the silk of silkworms that live in the wild anymore. People raise the silkworms. The silkworms are fed. The cocoons are kept safe. When the moths are close to coming out, the best cocoons are chosen. Those cocoons are saved, and the moths from them are used to lay new eggs. The other cocoons are baked in an oven. The next step is the silk-making process.

People only want the silk from the cocoons. The baked cocoons are placed in hot water. Then people use a brush to clean off the outside of each cocoon. At the same time they look for the beginnings of the long strings of silk. They are silk thread.

Silk thread is used to make silk cloth. Silk cloth is used to make many things. Silk is usually expensive. It costs so much because of the work and time needed to make silk. Also, a lot of silkworms are needed to make a small amount of silk. Would you believe over 600 cocoons are used to make one shirt? More than 100 cocoons are needed to make a necktie.

The next time you go to the store, look for items that are made of silk. Think about all the work that went into making each item—by both people and silkworms.